The ABCs of Christmas

*A Look at Holiday Traditions in
Canada and Around the World*

With Holiday Symbols & Interpretations, a Message of Peace,
a "To Learn More" Section and Educational Activities

By

MARI MALATZY
B.Com, B.Ed and OCT

Copyright © 2017 Mari Malatzy.

All rights reserved. No part of this book may be used or reproduced by any means, graphic, electronic, or mechanical, including photocopying, recording, taping or by any information storage retrieval system without the written permission of the author except in the case of brief quotations embodied in critical articles and reviews.

iUniverse books may be ordered through booksellers or by contacting:

iUniverse
1663 Liberty Drive
Bloomington, IN 47403
www.iuniverse.com
1-800-Authors (1-800-288-4677)

Because of the dynamic nature of the Internet, any web addresses or links contained in this book may have changed since publication and may no longer be valid. The views expressed in this work are solely those of the author and do not necessarily reflect the views of the publisher, and the publisher hereby disclaims any responsibility for them.

Any people depicted in stock imagery provided by Thinkstock are models,
and such images are being used for illustrative purposes only.
Certain stock imagery © Thinkstock.

ISBN: 978-1-5320-3911-9 (sc)
ISBN: 978-1-5320-3913-3 (hc)
ISBN: 978-1-5320-3912-6 (e)

Library of Congress Control Number: 2017918744

Print information available on the last page.

iUniverse rev. date: 12/20/2017

Dedications:

To my darling family who inspire me to be creative – thanks kids for telling me you like my stories.

To my first art instructor, Mr. P Callaghan, who always showed faith in his students.

To my cousin Mike who has always been supportive and encouraging to everyone he loves.

Note to Parents and Teachers:

Mari holds a Bachelor of Commerce Degree and a Bachelor of Education Degree. She has also been a classroom teacher for almost two decades, with experience in both elementary and secondary school. As a teacher, Mari Malatzy has found that students engage in the process of learning more when they find the material interesting and fun.

To parents and teachers interested in adding an educational component to a child's general reading experience, this book achieves that goal. The fun educational follow-ups at the end of the book are designed to further a child's imagination and encourage additional learning opportunities. Parents and teachers can choose to read a letter daily leading up to Christmas, followed by a selected educational activity. Reading one letter per day is a good way to chunk the material and allow for time to complete the suggested educational follow-up activity.

Younger kids may prefer to read the first part of the letters as the writing style is typically more simplistic and focused on common Christmas rituals and symbols. Older kids may wish to use the paragraphs about specific places as a general introduction or springboard to a research project. While the book's content will provide a child with information about Christmas traditions in Canada and around the world, the educational follow-ups will provide activities designed for a child's different learning needs. While some children may excel in art and design, others may prefer testing their language skills by writing about the nouns and verbs from their reading.

"A" is for Angel and Artificial Tree

Angels sing "Alleluia" atop an artificial tree,
Above Jesus, three wise men and the nativity.
People acting their best, spreading Christmas cheer,
Acceptance is important at this time of year.

Acorn and advent crafts are things you can make,
Quilts can be made and cookies can be baked.
While attention is paid to making spirits lift,
Albertans spend the most on buying Christmas gifts.

Christmas can be expensive and hard to afford,
The grateful bless meals and say "Amen" to the Lord.
Canadian Christmas meals are influenced by The U.S and U.K,
With foods like mashed potatoes, apple pie, ham or turkey.

Anne Murray's Christmas album may be tradition,
Canadians gather to give them a listen.
Nappanee, Ontario is home to Avril Lavigne,
Who worked on a Christmas album in 2015.

Calgary, Alberta's Brewster Adventures has sleigh rides to do,
Christmas cowboy meals, line dancing and an Ice Fall view.
Airdrie, Alberta has a Christmas Light show,
With a five acre park set completely aglow.

The Argentine Christmas ends on January 6th,
Up to Three Kings Day is when children get their gifts.
Instead of stockings, Argentine kids leave shoes,
Hay and some water for the Three Wise Men too.

The Australian Christmas ends on January 6th,
Families have a picnic with ham and salad mix.
Some Aussies use the barbie at the beach Christmas Day,
Father Christmas visits the beach for the holiday.

Angels are a sign of God's light and celebration.
Artificial trees - His everlasting life and creation.
Advent is Latin for *coming* and a symbol of preparation.
Acorns are a sign that small is great and a sign of our salvation.

Before your next poem, before the next page in the book,
Can you spot the words with "A"? – Will you take a good look?
There are *angels* and *artificial* to name but a few,
Amen, *advent*, *acorn*, and *album* are on that list too.

"B" is for Blizzard and Bell

Through Bolton, Brampton and Bracebridge, blizzards fiercely blow.
Canadians greet the winter with storms and snow.
Canadians who avoid snow, sleet, and slush,
Buy on-line to get around the Black Friday rush.

Canadians who feel their stuff is a bore,
May buy a new table from The Brick store.
Bettering the home for the holiday,
Hosting a traditional Christmas buffet.

Buying from the Bulk Barn to save a little bit,
Freshly baked cookies – on the table they will sit.
Pricey brie cheese and berries to try,
Bursting at the seams from all that was fried.

Big boots in Bracebridge, Ontario is common for snow,
Home to SantaFest and its beautiful light show.
Many of the Reindeer call Santa's Village their summer home,
This national park has 60 acres of nature to roam.

Brampton, Ontario has Christmas light shows and ice rinks,
A Christmas market, fire pits and hot chocolate drinks.
Burlington, Ontario celebrates Christmas in neat ways,
Their Christmas waterfront light show lasts up to 40 days.

Canadians like *The Nutcracker* from *The National Ballet*,
And the capital city's BeaverTails and street light displays.
Some wait for Christmas Eve to give boxes with bows,
Others attend Midnight Mass and fill the church's rows.

Toronto's Church bells of Bond Street ring: "Bing, Bong, Bing,"
Midnight mass is when St. Michael's Choir Boys sing.
Bible stories read of a special baby's birth,
Christ was brought here to save the people of the earth.

Bells are a symbol of God's guidance, marked by the ring.
Bows symbolize togetherness, a tie that goodwill brings.
A blizzard's snow is a sign of cleanliness and purity.
Black Friday is a symbol of a merchant's security.

Before your next poem, before the next page in the book,
Can you spot the words with "B"? – Will you take a good look?
There are *Brampton*, *Bracebridge*, and *blizzards* to name but a few,
Boxes, *bells*, *bows* and *BeaverTails* are on that list too.

"C" is for Christmas and Candy Cane

What is included in a Christmas celebration?
How about Christmas crackers and crafty creations?
Carolers singing and chestnuts roasting,
Parties with friends and glasses toasting.

Stockings for Mr. Claus by the cozy chimney fire,
Moms and dads sit and sip a hot chocolate or cider.
Candy cane decorations sit atop the tall Christmas tree,
The cinnamon scented candles set alight for all to see.

View *Christmas Carol* or *A Charlie Brown Christmas* on the CBC,
Or catch Canadian sports like curling on the good old T.V.
Canadian Tire ads sell things like shovels and boats,
Canucks battle the chill with Canada Goose coats.

Sending Christmas cards through Canada Post,
Calling cards are used to call those loved most.
Canadians buy from Le Chateau or Chapters book stores,
Canadians use credit cards for charities they trust more.

Toronto Ontario's Casa Loma has a look-out tower to the city,
10 designer Christmas trees make the castle more pretty.
This Gothic castle has 98 rooms and secret passageways too,
The conservatory hosts Santa photos and crafts kids can do.

At B.C.'s Capilano Suspension Bridge Park at night,
The Canyon and Cliffwalk turn into a festival of lights.
Here, dressed in glitter for all to see,
Are the world's largest living Christmas trees.

Christmas is a symbol of Christ's birth and the joy that He brings.
Crackers originated in the UK and are packed with jokes and things.
Carolers bring merriment and spread some good cheer, for the solstice and the longest night of the year.
Candy canes have two colours - white and red, to symbolize Christ's purity and the blood that He shed.

Before your next poem, before the next page in the book,
Can you spot the words with "C"? – Will you take a good look?
There are *Christmas*, *crackers*, and *carolers* to name but a few,
Candy cane, *candles* and *Christmas cards* are on that list too.

"D" is for December and Donation

December 25th is a special part of the year,
When time is spent with those you hold dear.
Families watch *The Little Drummer Boy*,
Children happily play with their new dreamy Toys.

Many have ham, chicken, turkey or duck for dinner,
And worry, in the New Year, about getting thinner.
Diets are common at the start of the New Year,
After donuts, dinner and much holiday cheer.

Canucks enjoy a Christmas store front display,
And sing songs like "Frere Jacque" en francais.
Dollar stores are home to crafty inspirations,
Making dazzling and darling Christmas creations.

Designing décor with a Christmas theme,
White doves are a common holiday scene.
Dasher and Dancer partake in reindeer games,
"Deck the Halls" is a famous Christmas song name.

The Atlantic region makes the message of charity clear,
Nova Scotia has *Stuff-A-Bus* with donations each year.
The Dalplex Christmas Craft Market has many treats,
Like pottery, wooden toys and delicious eats.

At Canada's Dalhousie University,
There are studies on benefits to real Christmas trees.
Bought at a farm or Toronto, Ontario's Distillery,
Is the dazzlingly dreamy real life Christmas tree.

Children enjoy Brampton, Ontario's Downey's Farm,
For Santa visits, crafts, photos and lunch in the barn.
Toronto's Distillery District has Christmas things to do,
With a life-sized gingerbread home and Ferris wheel too.

December 25th is a symbolic day that represents Jesus' birth.
The white dove symbolizes peace and The Holy Spirit on earth.
"Deck the Halls" symbolizes decorating and is of Welsh origination.
The Drummer Boy symbolizes Jesus' acceptance and His invitation.

Before your next poem, before the next page in the book,
Can you spot the words with "D"? – Will you take a good look?
There are *December, drummer* and *dove* to name but a few,
Dreamy, décor and *donations* are on that list too.

"E" is for Elf and Evergreen

Eh! Do you display an evergreen tree,
At Christmas in your home for all to see?
Expensive gifts are bought and sold,
Given to those with a heart of gold.

People come over with strong family ties,
Gifts are exchanged and expectations high.
No one wants to be seen as Ebenezer Scrooge,
So, of course, some people are urged to spend huge.

Some enjoy epic isles and endless shelves,
And line up for photos with Santa and his elves.
Some take a break with Eggnog – so hot and steamy,
Sold at Second Cup - so rich and so creamy.

Some think Christmas is an exhausting pain,
Others love having guests to entertain.
Children wonder about Santa letters and emails too,
Canada Post elves have sorted Santa mail since 1982.

Canada's customs are from each and every part of the globe,
The English celebrate Father Christmas and his long, red robes.
Some Europeans enjoy the Epiphany on January 6th,
This is also an old calendar day when many get their gifts.

Toronto's Eaton Centre is where tourists will go,
To see the Canada geese sculpture from Michael Snow.
At Christmas, the tree here is 100 feet tall,
One of the biggest trees to be seen in a mall.

For Edmonton homes who decorate dearly,
Thousands of visitors come visit yearly.
Guests use horse and carriage or simply walk,
Through Candy Cane Lane and its eight city blocks.

Evergreen trees are a symbol of life and God's connection to earth.
The Epiphany is a symbol of light to the world 12 days after Jesus' birth.
Eggnog is a symbol of wealth used to toast the dinner hour.
Elves are a symbol of German myth and magical powers.

Before your next poem, before the next page in the book,
Can you spot the words with "E"? – Will you take a good look?
There are *evergreen*, *elves*, and *eggnog* to name but a few,
Epiphany and *Europeans* are on that list too.

"F" is for Father Christmas and Frankincense

The heavenly king - finally born,
God's only son in human form.
The king receives frankincense,
From three men with presents.

Churches recount the nativity,
And faith fills the hearts of families.
Families fine dine in fancy attire,
And expect Father Christmas by the fire.

After many festivities, families like to retire,
With a cup of hot cocoa by a cozy Christmas fire.
Figgy pudding and fruitcake are common foods,
To help people stay in a good Christmas mood.

For India, Poland, Romania and Spain,
Fruitcake comes after the Christmas main.
In Canada, the fruitcake is a Christmas cake,
Like in the UK, it is bread loaf shaped.

"Feliz Navidad" is what the Spanish say,
Said before and said during Christmas day.
A frosted man kids make with snow,
Three snowballs used to make him grow.

The West Coast has fabulous scenery, snowy and nice -
Celebrate Christmas in a snowmobiler's paradise.
Dog sled or ski the frosted forests of The Canadian Rockies,
Fort McMurray has the perfect weather to hike or to play hockey.

Fredericton, New Brunswick is close to the home of singer Stompin Tom,
A place with fiddles, light houses and tremendous maritime charm.
Fredericton Boyce Farmer's Market is known to this city,
A Saturday market with Christmas gifts - handmade and pretty.

Frankincense is a perfume, a symbol of the Divine's name to the living.
Fruitcake is enjoyed by the monarchy, a symbol of holiday giving.
A frosted white snowman is a symbol of purity and the love of a child.
Father Christmas is a symbol of reward to children who behave and smile.

Before your next poem, before the next page in the book,
Can you spot the words with "F"? – Will you take a good look?
There are *frankincense*, *fruitcake* and *fancy* to name but a few,
Faith, *frosted*, *Father Christmas* and *families* are on that list too.

"G" is for Gingerbread and Goodwill

Gluttony hits every now and then,
So "God Rest Ye Merry Gentlemen".
In each house, great food is put aside,
Like glasses of milk for Santa inside.

Decorated houses await Christmas guests,
With garlands and gifts and holiday bests.
Gingerbread homes made of candy,
And store gift cards come in handy.

Many stress about cooking the holiday goose,
And what to serve with it – gravy or au jus.
The green and gold cloths cover the table,
And *Home Alone* airs later on cable.

Christmas is a time for goodwill and giving,
Giving you a purpose to how you are living.
Stores give away things to those in need,
To encourage us all to minimize greed.

For years, Ed Mirvish bought turkeys for his Toronto store,
For Thanksgiving and Christmas, he gave to the poor.
We learn a thing from men just like this,
Giving gives you the sense of holiday bliss.

"O Tannenbaum" the Germans may sing,
Glory be to Christkind – the newborn king.
German Christmas markets fill the hearts of their cities,
Filled with glittery glass lights - so neat and so pretty.

"Kala Christouyenna" is what the Greeks say,
As a holiday greeting near Christmas day.
Greeks enjoy homemade St. Basil's Day cake,
And money is hidden in a piece that is baked.

Garland is a symbol of what is on a wreath and a circle of unity.
Gingerbread is a symbol of the creation of man for all to see.
Gold is a symbol of wealth and kings - a known holiday colour.
Goodwill is an important symbol of God's will and love for others.

Before your next poem, before the next page in the book,
Can you spot the words with "G"? – Will you take a good look?
There are *guests, garlands* and *gifts* to name but a few,
Gingerbread, green, gold and *goodwill* are on that list too.

"H" is for Holly and Holiday

Christmas movies are part of holiday traditions,
Some filmed in Canada's wintery conditions.
Hollywood North in *The Christmas Story* is cool,
In it you see TTC cars and Ralphie's school.

Canucks host *Hockey Night in Canada* – a winter thing to do,
CBC has shown Gretzky, Orr and Howie since 1952.
Drinking hot cocoa and watching hockey in the stands,
Happy parents watch their kids play the game of the land.

Holiday portraits with Santa hats on dogs,
Hand holding couples with a background of logs.
Whether its holly or Hanukkah bliss,
Albertans spend more on holiday gifts.

Hearts are filled with happy thoughts when,
"Hark! The Herald Angels Sing" again.
London's Harrods and Toronto's Hudson's Bay,
Have the best Christmas store front window displays.

The Home Shopping Network – a place to spend money,
On buying nice gifts for him or his honey.
The Heft is placed on a shovel to help lift the snow,
A Canadian product from The Dragons' Den show.

Holidays are a time to say "Thank you dear,
For all the kind things you have done this year."
Halifax's Christmas tree send-off says "Thank you" each year,
To Boston for their help in a disastrous fire they feared.

People show heart and tend to give thanks,
By fundraising for hunger and food banks.
Hamilton's CP Holiday Train is hundreds of feet long,
It raises money with 14 rail cars of music and song.

Holidays symbolize family time and how a celebration is led.
Holly and its red berry symbolize eternal life and Christ's bloodshed.
Hanukkah is a symbol of dedication, a Jewish light fest - 8 days long.
Hockey is a symbol of Canada, its weather and the true north strong.

Before your next poem, before the next page in the book,
Can you spot the words with "H"? – Will you take a good look?
There are *holiday*, *home* and *happy* to name but a few,
Holly, *Hanukkah* and *hockey* are on that list too.

"I" is for Ivy and Ice

Innocent Jesus lay in the scene of nativity,
His infant birth the cause of Christmas festivity.
An invitation to increase the message of love,
From the heavenly Father who resides above.

In many homes at Christmas, ivy is found,
It clings to an object and grows from the ground.
It is a symbol of our need for God's support,
His love for all of us brings much peace and comfort.

Many use ivy and holly for home décor,
Common products you can find in most stores.
While some see Christmas as a time to decorate,
Others enjoy ice and strap on the skates.

Houses around the globe are illuminated with care,
In hopes that St. Nicholas will find his way there.
While some watch *It's a Wonderful Life* on the IMAX,
Others fill their homes with scented candles and wax.

Some Irish folk believe in the power of light,
A candle by the window on Christmas Eve night.
A special person should ignite the candle's flame,
Representing travellers, Mary should be her name.

Some Canadians live in houses, tents and igloos,
Aboriginal Christmas includes fish and caribou stews.
Muktuk is what the Inuit eat,
Whale skin blubber - a raw Christmas treat.

Some Italians feast on seven types of fish,
And say "Buon Natale" as a Christmas wish.
La Befana is the Epiphany witch that takes flight,
Italians believe she delivers toys through the night.

The green Ivy is a symbol of rebirth, the spring season and vitality.
The window candle symbolizes a traveller's lit path and hospitality.
Ice is a symbol of someone's cold heart and cold winter solstice days.
Illumination symbolizes lighting a life up in some way.

Before your next poem, before the next page in the book,
Can you spot the words with "I"? – Will you take a good look?
There are *innocent*, *infant* and *invitation* to name but a few,
Ivy, *ice*, *illumination* and *Irish* are on that list too.

"J" is for Jesus and Jack Frost

What is the meaning of the Christmas season?
Jesus is the man behind it - he is the reason.
Jolly old St. Nick spreads the power of God's word,
Rewarding joyful good deeds – God's message is heard.

Just as the tales of Christmas begin to unfold,
Jack Frost shows he is the King of the Cold.
Joy is felt down the hill on a sled,
Jumping and sliding on a snow bed.

"Jingle Bells" is a famous song today,
About one horse and an open sleigh.
A good movie to catch is *Jingle all The Way*,
A dad on a mission for a toy Christmas day.

"Joyeux Noel" is what the French say,
Before and during Christmas day.
Join Christmas with a French-Canadian feel,
Add bacon pea soup or meat tarts to your meal.

Jackets on this Christmas – join the cool club,
Jacques – Cartier, Quebec is a winter outdoor hub.
Nordic spas and hot tubs with crisp mountain views,
Tour *Aventure Inukshuk* to see black bears too.

With jagged mountain peaks and lessons on geology,
Jasper, Alberta has The Canadian Rockies.
Join Jasper's National Park for nature hikes,
Or just thrill seek if it is an ice climb you'd like.

The Fairmont Jasper Park Lodge says it is okay,
To swim outside in the winter on a very cold day.
View the snow covered mountains and trees,
In the pool that remains heated at 88 degrees.

Jesus Christ is a symbol of salvation and praise.
Jack Frost is a symbol of very cold weather days.
Jolly Old St. Nick is a symbol of merriment and joy.
Jingle Bells is a symbol of Christmas for girls and boys.

Before your next poem, before the next page in the book,
Can you spot the words with "J"? – Will you take a good look?
There are *Jesus, joy* and *Jack Frost* to name but a few,
Jumping, "*Jingle Bells*" and *jackets* are on that list too.

"K" is for Krampus and Kris Kringle

The kingdom of heaven is filled with His glory,
Christ the King's lessons are told in bible stories.
Through parables and miracles – Jesus would preach,
Kindness and forgiveness is what he would teach.

Kris Kringle, the person, checks his naughty list twice,
He knows if and when children are naughty or nice.
You know he is coming with his sleigh bells,
Kids will get presents when they behave well.

Kris Kringle, the custom, is a gift-giving game,
From a hat, you select someone's name.
It could be coworkers, family or even a friend,
Who gets the gift you, the Secret Santa, will send.

Kris Kringle is a German name for Santa Claus too,
Many Germans live in Ontario's Kitchener-Waterloo.
Some German's believe in Krampus and his image stays in their brains,
This scary monster visits at Christmas with coal, bells and chains.

Kitchener's old city hall has gifts for everyone,
The origin of Canada's Christmas market fun.
Markets set up in a real European way,
They run four days long, into the night and all day.

A mistletoe kiss from a girl to a boy,
At a Christmas tent with small wooden toys.
The Kitchener Christmas Market is a big thing,
Dancers entertain and musical guests sing.

Kingston, Ontario is Canada's first capital city,
Home to Queens University and a campus that is pretty.
The Kingston Trolley Tour is 90 minutes long,
Viewing Christmas downtown while caroling along.

Kingdom is a symbol of God's rule and eternal life with Him,
King is a symbol of truth and power - He saves people from sin.
Kris Kringle symbolizes Santa and gift giving.
The Krampus monster symbolizes life without thanksgiving.

Before your next poem, before the next page in the book,
Can you spot the words with "K"? – Will you take a good look?
There are *kingdom*, *king*, and *kindness* to name but a few,
Kris Kringle, *knows*, *kids*, *Krampus* and *kiss* are on that list too.

"L" is for Light and Log Fire

In the Gospel of Matthew, there glows a bright light,
The star of Bethlehem shines through the night.
Three men use this light to find their way,
To the little Lord Jesus on Christmas day.

To be reminded of the Lord and what matters most,
Lights are lit for Christmas at the home of the host.
Lights are strung around the home and Christmas tree,
A symbol of renewal, new life and clarity.

Children laughing loudly as they lazily play,
With the long list of toys they got Christmas day.
The Lord says it is better to give than to receive,
But for many at Christmas, there is the label of greed.

At Christmas, some leisurely walk in paths of snow,
Singing: "Fa La La La La" with lanterns that glow.
Christmas is a time for love - not lists, gifts or greed,
Help the less fortunate and give to those in need.

"I am heading up to the lake" - a Canadian phrase,
Christmas at the lake may mean lazy log fire days.
Cross-country paths and snowshoe trails are praised,
At Lake Louise, Alberta for the holidays.

Lake Louise has alpine World Cup ski racing– of course,
Which is a reason thrill seekers stay at the local resorts.
Since 1984, international teams here have had a mission,
To win The Ice Magic Festival's ice carving competition.

Louisbourg, Nova Scotia is another tourist attraction,
The Fortress of Louisbourg once had military action.
France's King Louis felt this port had the best cod fishing around,
In the winter, many stroll the paths of this reconstructed town.

Lights and candles at Christmas are a symbol of Christ – the guide of our world – His light.
The Lord is believed to be a master of people and is a symbol of power and might.
Laughter is a symbol of a positive emotional state – shown with a happy face.
Logs are a symbol of warmth and a very cozy, comfortable place.

Before your next poem, before the next page in the book,
Can you spot the words with "L"? – Will you take a good look?
There are *light, little, Lord,* and *laughing* to name but a few,
Long list, lanterns, love and *log fire* are on that list too.

"M" is for Myrrh and Mistletoe

The magic of Christmas began long ago,
With the miracle birth of a baby we know.
The Virgin Mary was filled with joy,
Jesus in the manger was her baby boy.

The Magi gave gold and myrrh among other things,
Glory be given to this new magical king.
"Merry Christmas" is now what they say,
To celebrate the Messiah's birthday.

Kids line up to give Mr. and Mrs. Claus a hug,
Christmas cards on the mantel and eggnog in their mugs.
Mistletoes in doorways for all to see,
Manufactured toys sitting under a tree.

Many shop the mall during this magical time,
Buying Christmas mitts, mince pie and mulled wine.
Mall music and mascots create buying moods,
So money is spent on the markets and food.

Making stylish Christmas gifts with world-wide demand,
Is Manitobah – a Canadian footwear brand.
This Canadian company has strong aboriginal roots,
Making Manitobah Mukluks - warm winter boots.

Many watch *Miracle on 34th Street* air on the CBC,
While families gather in the kitchen to make Christmas turkey.
The midnight meal is part of Filipino hospitality,
"Noche Buena" is a feast believed to bring prosperity.

Many feel the magic of Christmas is tied to the snow,
So the Muskoka area may be the place to go.
Mew Lake Campground has modern roofed yurts and winter tents,
Mount St. Louis Moonstone has 36 slopes to experience.

The miracle birth is a symbol of God's love for the human race.
Mary is Jesus' mother - a symbol of God's saving grace.
Mistletoe, thought to ward off evil, is a symbol of peace and fertility.
Myrrh symbolizes suffering – and is a medicine from the gum of a tree.

Before your next poem, before the next page in the book,
Can you spot the words with "M"? – Will you take a good look?
There are *miracle, manger* and *Mary* to name but a few,
Myrrh, messiah, mistletoes and *magical* are on that list too.

"N" is for St. Nick and North Pole

Along with gifts at the foot of the tree,
Is a nativity scene for all to see.
Around the world, people often display,
This symbol of Jesus on Christmas day.

Old St. Nick lives in the nippy North Pole,
Making nice presents is one of his goals.
Naughty kids are deprived of the toys,
Only reserved for nice girls and boys.

The Nutcracker Ballet shows a famous Christmas scene,
A winter land, Sugar Plum Fairy, and Snow Queen.
NORAD is The North American Aerospace Defence Command,
It helps track Santa, his sleigh and where he goes through the land.

For Christmas, many Quebecers like to bake,
A tasty "Bûche de Noël" or yule log cake.
Nova Scotians eat lobster and shell fish,
A common East Coast Christmas Eve dish.

Newfoundland and Nova Scotia are interesting places,
Locals ring door bells and wear masks on their faces.
This East Coast custom has people acting in odd ways,
Mummers do this annually for the 12 Christmas days.

Some join Newfoundland's Avalon Peninsula for their Festival of Lights,
And go to two Santa Claus parades - one in the day and another at night.
Newfoundland's Bay Roberts has national awards for the light show,
The large nativity collection and live scene sets the night aglow.

"One of the world's natural wonders" is what some call,
The majestically beautiful views of Niagara Falls.
Niagara Falls strings over three million lights through the city,
With Christmas fireworks at The Falls- so cold, but so pretty.

St. Nick is often another name for Santa and a symbol of gift giving.
Nativity is a symbol of Jesus' birth – He who comes to save the living.
The Nutcracker is a German symbol of protection and goodwill.
The North Pole is a symbol of Santa, his elves and his magic toy mill.

Before your next poem, before the next page in the book,
Can you spot the words with "N"? – Will you take a good look?
There is *nativity*, and *St. Nick* to name but a few,
North Pole, *Nutcracker* and *NORAD* are on that list too.

"O" is for Ornament and Occasion

Christmas is a time for observance and thought,
Not just a time to dwell on things that are bought.
Christmas is a time to reflect on what matters the most,
For peace and love are gifts from our most heavenly host.

Christmas is not just a time to overfill on food and open gifts,
It is time to settle offences and own up to our rifts.
This is an occasion to be overjoyed and happy,
Not a time to oppose others and be snarky and snappy.

Some buy gifts and shop on-line,
To replace outgrown clothes and order wine.
Forget the Christmas obligation, stress and trouble,
Buy on-sale items and do not pay double.

Some open only one gift on Christmas Eve night,
Others think it is the time to open all gifts in sight.
Some decorate an outdated tree with ribbon and strings,
Others use ornaments shaped like birds that can sing.

Ottawa, Ontario oozes with Christmas cheer,
Chalets sell BeaverTails and maple taffy each year.
Canada's Prime Minister often flicks the lights on,
To Parliament Hill's Christmas show with music and song.

As you skate and slide along Ottawa's Rideau Canal,
See Parliament Hill and Fairmont Chateau Laurier Hotel.
Ottawa's Winterlude Festival and sculptures are quite nice,
The Rideau Canal Skateway is like 90 Olympic rinks of ice.

Orangeville, Ontario can be an extremely festive place too,
The Credit Valley Explorer train ride can be a thing to do.
Santa will visit with gingerbread while you ride the 74 km rail,
The train has classic cars that ride through snowy scenic trails.

Opening gifts symbolizes celebrating the perfect gift of God's son.
Observance symbolizes coming home to Church to reflect on The Holy One.
Occasions symbolize spending special time with those you love.
Ornaments of white doves symbolize peace and joy from above.

Before your next poem, before the next page in the book,
Can you spot the words with "O"? – Will you take a good look?
There are *observance*, and *occasion* to name but a few,
Open, *obligation* and *ornaments* are on that list too.

"P" is for Poinsettia and Parade

People pray and reflect on Christmas and its meaning,
Some spend Christmas in search of a spiritual cleaning.
The Pope sends a message from the Lord above,
Praising all those who show unity and love.

Parents praise kids performing in a pageant or play,
About the town of Bethlehem and Jesus' birthday.
Proud parents pack the plazas to find the perfect toy,
Taking photos and sending pictures of their girl or boy.

Poinsettias and plants are in doorways for a Christmas event,
People at parties bring packaged cookies, pies and presents.
Prancer and pals visit on Christmas Eve and on the roof they will stay,
Until all the puppets, puzzles and play centres are unpacked from the sleigh.

Chileans eat "Pan de Pascua" and Italians eat "Panettone",
Others like plum pudding, pumpkin pie, or tea and scones.
After dinner, many may sit down to watch parades on TV,
While singers sing phrases like "A Partridge in a Pear Tree."

Harry Potter and Hockey Night in Canada floats in sight,
At Toronto, Ontario's Santa Parade – a yearly delight.
With about 2000 participants in costumes and coats,
It has over 100 years of proud tradition and floats.

Some enjoy Christmas in a paid for package holiday,
When the panic of hosting a party is simply taken away.
Some Canucks partake in Christmas in a cabin or National Park,
Tobogganing or snowshoeing on park paths from morning till dark.

Christmas can be spent in Jasper, Alberta's Pyramid Lake,
Oversized tires allow Fatbikes on the snowy paths they take.
Churchill, Manitoba is another interesting place to see,
Spot the polar bears on a slow moving Tundra Buggy.

The leaves of the poinsettia are a symbol of the star that led the three wise men.
"A Partridge in a Pear Tree" is a symbol of Jesus Christ and the cross made then.
Plum Pudding is a symbol of Jesus and his disciples - a 13 ingredient recipe.
Parades are a symbol of what is celebrated as a cultural necessity.

Before your next poem, before the next page in the book,
Can you spot the words with "P"? – Will you take a good look?
There are *pray*, *pageant* and *parades* to name but a few,
Poinsettias, *Prancer* and *plum pudding* are on that list too.

"Q" is for Quebec and Quality Street

Christmas is a time for kids to be out of school,
No tests or quizzes, no teachers or rules.
Since Santa may question if a kid is good or bad,
Kids need to quit quarrelling or no gifts will be had.

Some attend Christmas Eve mass to quietly pray,
Jesus is the quintessential part of their holiday.
Feeling a need to quench a thirst for religion,
Attending mass may fix that feeling a smidgen.

A quest for prayer during Christmas' Midnight Mass,
Enjoy the gothic church paintings and stain glass.
Quebec's Notre Dame Basilica is decorated with gold,
This Canadian historic site is over 300 years old.

Many watch TV and munch on Holiday treats,
Such as Hershey chocolates and Quality Street.
The Queen's speech is aired on a quiet Christmas day,
With a quick message of peace she would like to say.

Many Quebecers prepare Christmas feasts and buy,
Traditional pig legs for stew and a savoury meat pie.
After a quaint quality meal with quirky guests at dark,
Stroll Quebec's cobblestone walkways and its wintry parks.

Minutes away from downtown Quebec City,
Is a unique hotel - so grand and so pretty.
Made of ice and snow, Hotel de Glace is very neat,
The 44 rooms are themed - like Disney's Frozen suite.

This Christmas, buy tickets for a Cirque Du Soleil show –
The 1980s Quebec street performers made this show known?
Some enjoy the holidays exploring paths on a snowmobile machine,
A Quebecer, Joseph Bombardier, invented the snowmobile at age 15.

Quebec's Notre Dame Basilica is a Cathedral and a symbol of catholic unification.
Quality Street Chocolate is a symbol of an affordable luxury for many generations.
The Queen's message is a symbol of a commonwealth unity mission.
Quebec City is a symbol of bilingualism and European traditions.

Before your next poem, before the next page in the book,
Can you spot the words with "Q"? – Will you take a good look?
There are *quizzes*, *question*, and *Queen* to name but a few,
Quench, *Quebec* and *quality* are on that list too.

"R" is for Ritual and Reindeer

Jesus may be the real reason,
For rejoicing Christmas season.
For some, Christmas means religious reflection,
Reunions, rituals and ready gift selections.

Churches recite Christmas bible reads too,
Reminding everyone of what they should do.
Remove rage and react with peace and love,
Act in a manner like the Redeemer above.

Reactions to Christmas differ around the globe,
Some choose to use rituals that are very old.
A Holy Supper with 12 dishes is what Russians eat,
At Christmas, it is a reminder of each apostle's feats.

Christmas is a special time of the year,
Refuge is taken in relations held dear.
Gatherings around a real Christmas tree,
Decorated with red ribbons for all to see.

Kids race to bed Christmas Eve night,
Hoping to hear the red sleigh in flight.
Rudolph's bright red nose lights up the sky,
So Santa's reindeer are safe when they fly.

Reindeer are able to see through snowstorms,
Rudolph's rooftop landings are a Christmas norm.
Rudolph, The Red Nose Reindeer has a Canadian connection,
The 1964 movie had Canadian actor selection.

Some travel with friends at Christmas to a place that is new,
Canada's Castle in The Rockies may be the thing to do.
Banff, Alberta has Canada's oldest national park and hotels too,
Surrounded by ice fields, forests and landscapes – what a nice view!

Red is a symbol of Christ and the blood He shed for our sins on the cross.
Rudolph's red nose is a symbol of Christ and how he gives light to those lost.
Reindeer are a symbol of nature's pure at heart who have the gift of real sight.
The Rocky Mountains are a symbol of nearness to God due to their height.

Before your next poem, before the next page in the book,
Can you spot the words with "R"? – Will you take a good look?
There are *red*, *Rudolph*, and *religious* to name but a few,
Reunions, *rituals* and *reindeer* are on that list too.

"S" is for Stocking and Santa

Silver bells strung along the many Christmas trees,
Snow atop the mountains of the great old Rockies.
Season's greetings from Santa at the North Pole,
Sounds, spices and smells of Christmas you know.

Yearly snowfalls can be hated, but some find it pretty,
About 12 feet of snow falls in Labrador City.
When the storms hit and the snowfall is big,
Canucks shovel the snow and dig, dig, dig!

Scarves and sweaters, warm as can be,
Building a snowman for all to see.
Slip on some skis, skates or snowshoes,
Sledding and sliding the whole day through.

Shell Gas fills cars before a shop in the city,
Shops filled with sounds and smells that are pretty.
After a shop for Christmas sales and holiday steals,
Canucks like Second Cup or Swiss Chalet Meals.

Stocking stuffers like socks fill up the cart,
At the good old local Shoppers Drug Mart.
Stores like this one let people save huge,
Without feeling like a heartless scrooge.

Canada has an interesting statistic,
Stores who noticed became opportunistic.
Canada's Saskatoon has the most kids under 14 years old,
Which clearly results in more candy and toys sold.

There is Simcoe Christmas Panorama River of Lights,
With over 50 years of winter wonderlands at night.
Christmas in Ontario water has sparkling floats,
As well as energy efficient lights on the boats.

Silver bells symbolize a flower on a tree.
Santa is a symbol of generosity.
Scrooge is a symbol of one who is greedy, thoughtless and mean.
Stockings cover feet and symbolize being spiritually clean.

Before your next poem, before the next page in the book,
Can you spot the words with "S"? – Will you take a good look?
There are *silver bells* and *snow* to name but a few,
Santa, *Scrooge*, and *stocking* are on that list too.

"T" is for Tinsel and Toboggan

Tabernacles and temples teach about the Ultimate Truth,
A time for togetherness, friendship, families and youth.
Seasonal customs are passed on and on,
Through tranquil traditional hymns and song.

"The Twelve Days of Christmas" has a Catholic sentiment,
Two turtle doves represent the old and new testaments.
"Twas The Night Before Christmas" is a famous story,
About Santa, his reindeer, his toys, and his glory.

Good tidings for those in the Christmas mood,
Turkey and trimmings and tons of good food.
Tinsel and trinkets atop the tallest tree,
Tasty toasts and tables with holiday treats.

Stores tempt and tease shoppers with tremendously trendy selections,
Like the board game Trivial Pursuit - a Canadian invention.
Toys, teddy bears, truffles and toboggans too,
Whatever the gift, please text or say, "Thank you."

Toronto, Ontario's Christmas Cavalcade of Lights,
Includes fireworks, music and the tree lighting at night.
Crews take many hours to erect the large spruce tree,
For Toronto's Nathan Philips Square tree ceremony.

Toronto's Christmas tree is 18 meters tall,
1967's tree lighting showed off New City Hall.
Toronto's Santa Clause Parade is a top attraction,
Twinkling lights and terrific floats are part of the action.

The Christmas Market at Toronto's Distillery District is neat,
A perfect place for traditional gifts and handmade crafts and treats.
Here, Santa's House and The Elves workshop can be part of the day,
You can even ride the carousel or walk through Santa's laneway.

Turkey is a symbol of wholesome family food, annually a perfect part of the Christmas mood.
Toboggans are a symbol of transportation for some – an enjoyable activity for everyone.
Toys are a symbol of giving and sacrifice for those valued and loved.
Tinsel is a symbol of a simple offering valued by the Lord above.

Before your next poem, before the next page in the book,
Can you spot the words with "T"? – Will you take a good look?
There are *turkey* and *toboggans* to name but a few,
Tinsel, *tree* and *traditional* are on that list too.

"U" is for Unwrap and Universal Message

The bible unlocks the Christmas connection,
Jesus' story of unbelievable affection.
Bible stories unfold and tales of Jesus are told,
Christians feel united in the faith that they hold.

Christmas is a time to unleash the joy,
To undo the bows and unwrap the toys.
Santa unloads his toys and unpacks his sleigh,
Rewarding good children on Christmas day.

The universal Christmas message rings true,
Unite in kindness - it is the right thing to do!
Urging charitable giving to those in need,
Understanding there are other people to feed.

Unthaw the turkey hours before,
Unveil the gifts brought from the store.
Unlock the door for guests that come over,
Uncork the wine for those who are older.

Christmas is celebrated with different things,
Some Americans decorate trees with popcorn strings.
Ukrainians eat a special porridge made of wheat,
January 6th is the day for their 12 dish feast.

Ugly Christmas sweater events in Niagara on The Lake may be a lure,
Uncover the scenic town through a history walk or guided food tour.
Some Canadians would rather spend Christmas on a trip to The U.S.A.,
Visiting Florida for an unconventional Christmas holiday.

United States' New York City has the famous Rockefeller tree,
United States' Louisiana river bonfires help "Papa Noel" see.
United States' New England has impressive Christmas shops open all year long,
United States' Hawaii has Ukuleles for Christmas music and song.

Unwrapping toys is a symbol of joy for the giver who wants great reactions.
Ugly Christmas sweaters are a symbol of unique Christmas party attractions.
Urging charitable giving symbolizes Christmas' meaning, encouraged at schools.
The Universal Message of kindness is a symbol of Jesus and The Golden Rule.

Before your next poem, before the next page in the book,
Can you spot the words with "U"? – Will you take a good look?
There are *unwrap*, *ugly* and *universal* to name but a few,
Unite, *understanding* and *unveil* are on that list too.

"V" is for Vixen and Vacation

Visits made on a very special day,
Visualizing Jesus on his birthday.
Vowing that church is where you will spend,
Valuable time with family or friends.

Remember the voice of His holiness,
Vanish those feelings of loneliness.
Go to church in a suit or Christmas vest,
Try to act and look your very best.

Volunteer time so others feel better,
Try to help someone in snowy weather.
Shovel a driveway for someone who cannot do it,
Hold the mall door and help someone through it.

There are a vast number of things you can do,
And so much joy you can bring to someone too.
Show everyone that you have a heart of gold,
Visit your grandparents who may be very old.

Kind kids may be sure to catch a glimpse of Santa with Vixen,
Rudolf, Donner, Dancer, Prancer, Comet, Cupid and Blitzen.
Vacation safely at Christmas on the well-known Via Rail,
Venturing coast-to-coast through Canada's scenic trails.

Quebec's Village Vacances Valcartier has much to do,
With snow slides, indoor parks and skating trails too.
Vancouver's Stanley Park has a Christmas event called: "Bright Lights",
Families can buy a mini-train ride through the displays at night.

What did *Time* magazine say about Vancouver in 2002?
It was the birthplace of the first ugly sweater party - who knew?
Vancouver is also the birthplace of the great Michael Bublé,
A vocal chart topper who sings in a Sinatra kind of way.

Visiting at Christmas is a symbol of bonding and a personal connection.
Visualizing Jesus is a symbol of religious affiliation and affection.
A Christmas vest symbolizes atmosphere and looking good for the holiday.
Volunteering is a symbol of sacrifice and a personal nicety display.

Before your next poem, before the next page in the book,
Can you spot the words with "V"? – Will you take a good look?
There are *visits*, and *visualizing* to name but a few,
Vest, *Volunteer* and *Vixen* are on that list too.

"W" is for Winter and Wreath

Wise men walking on Christmas night,
Following a star shining bright.
Baby Jesus was the cause for their search,
Many wake Sunday to witness His church.

Wrapped gifts below the Christmas tree,
Wreaths on the doors for guests to see.
Advent wreaths on tables waiting to be lit,
And kids waiting and wishing for old St. Nick.

Some wander winter wonderlands nicely,
Some worry the weather is wickedly icy.
Watch those walking as ice wipeouts unfold,
Witness the white winter's snow - wildly cold.

At Christmas time, Canada may be covered in snow,
That is 30 feet high with temperatures 20 below.
When rushing last minute for wrapping paper and bows,
Some may find windshields of ice and cars buried in snow.

Windsor and Waterloo, Winnipeg and Whistler too,
When in Canada at Christmas, winter awaits you.
Wintertime exhibits and ice sculptures everywhere,
From Yorkville, Toronto to Quebec's Bonhomme affair.

Toronto, Ontario's Hudson Bay window displays,
May show a whimsical woodland scene for the holidays.
Winnipeg, Manitoba has the nation's largest holiday drive-thru,
2.5 km of themed light trails, skating rinks and sleigh rides too.

Whistler Blackcomb is a ski resort that is often ranked number one,
The 200 trails of snow and 8000 acres of slopes are sure to be fun.
West Edmonton Mall at Christmas has 800 stores to explore,
The world's largest lake and an amusement park indoors.

Wise Men are a symbol of interpretive skill and the scene of nativity.
White snow at Christmas is a symbol of Jesus and His purity.
The advent wreath candles symbolize penance, preparation, rejoicing and prayer.
Door Wreaths in the shape of a ring are a symbol of eternal strength and care.

Before your next poem, before the next page in the book,
Can you spot the words with "W"? – Will you take a good look?
There are *Wise, wrapped, wreaths* and *waiting* to name but a few,
Weather, white, winter and *wonderlands* are on that list too.

"X" is for Christmas and words with "EX"

EXperience the beauty of Xmas day,
EXcitement shown in a special way,
EXplaining how Jesus was born on this day,
EXamining the true message of the holiday.

Xmas is an EXpected time to be more giving,
A time to EXhibit love and be more forgiving.
Rearranging schedules to be more inclusive.
Making time for family, not being EXclusive.

EXhausted hosts fret about the Xmas mood,
Preparing EXaggerated amounts of food,
EXperiment with the new tasty sensations,
With EXtremely inventive meal creations.

EXpectations of a perfect day may be had,
EXtract the best parts of the day and be glad.
EXclude the moments that could make you mad,
EXecute the decision to be happy, not sad.

Christmas stores EXist for your shopping pleasure,
The malls are a place to EXit from the cold weather.
Niagara on The Lake has a Just Christmas store,
This all-year round shop has crafty ideas to EXplore.

Banff, Alberta has The Spirit of Christmas store,
With an EXact Christmas countdown and so much more.
EXit this store with wood carvings and snow globes too,
This Christmas store has stuff to EXcite and amaze you.

If you get a gift you would rather EXchange,
Do not act like you think the gift is strange.
EXercise caution before you say what is true,
EXtinguish the choice to be nasty and rude.

For some, *Xmas* is a symbol in the shortening of the "Christmas" word.
For some, when *Xmas* is written this way, the holiday purpose is blurred.
For some, *Xmas* symbolizes the Greek letter "X" or Chi for Christ, The Holy One.
In this way, *Xmas* symbolizes The Lord, The Saviour and The Holy Son.

Before your next poem, before the next page in the book,
Can you spot the words with "X"? – Will you take a good look?
There are *EXperience*, and *EXcitement* to name but a few,
EXpected, *EXist*, *EXplore* and *EXchange* are on that list too.

"Y" is for Yuletide and Yorkshire Pudding

Some fear the Christmas meaning is unclear,
As Christ may be the way of yester year.
Christmas is a celebration of baby Jesus' birth,
And the sacrifice He made for the people of earth.

"Yuletide" is "Christmas" – just said another way,
An Old English word for the holiday,
Yule is a common word in many songs and rhymes,
It can refer to the 12 day festival time.

Many seek comfort throughout the holidays,
Making Yorkshire pudding part of their festivities.
The yule log is lit to help feel warm,
The yellow glow of the fire is the norm.

At Christmas, kids yank closed their coats and go for the thrill,
Yelling and shouting while sledding down snow-covered hills.
Kids yearn for dog sled rides, skating and Santa photos too,
Parents yap over hot cider and the cookie decorating they do.

In Canada's Whitehorse, Yukon, kids play at Shipyards Park,
Enjoying Christmas themed activities from morning until dark.
The Yukon Territories hosts Santa Land and a festival of Lights.
Shipyards Park is where the action is from morning until late night.

In Canada, some enjoy winter camping in a yurt for the holiday,
Algonquin Provincial Park offers several yurts for people to stay.
Yurts are eight sided tents, mounted on a wooden floor,
6 campers can enjoy heat, electricity, bunk beds and more.

In Iceland, Christmas is special for all girls and boys,
Yule Lads leave bad kids potatoes and good kids fun toys.
Yawning kids leave shoes by the window for 13 days,
The costumed Yule Lads visit in a mischievous way.

Yuletide is a symbol of the many days leading up to Christmas day.
The Yule Log is a symbol of the Lord's light, His guidance and His way.
Yorkshire pudding is a symbol of the U.K.'s classic food holiday tradition.
The yellow colour of the fire is a symbol of happiness and illumination.

Before your next poem, before the next page in the book,
Can you spot the words with "Y"? – Will you take a good look?
There are *yuletide* and *Yorkshire pudding* to name but a few,
Yule log, *yellow* and *Yule Lads* are on that list too.

"Z" is for Zest and Zamboni

If Jesus is the center of the holiday,
Zoom on over to a church this Christmas day.
Zip through song pages, sung all month long,
Join zany people singing Christmas songs.

Zip the heavy coat that makes driving hard,
Zap to the drugstore for a Christmas card.
Zealous people with an interest to buy,
Zigzag in malls or shop on-line on the fly.

Zillions of to-do lists and mall shopping,
Zero energy left after store hopping.
Get into the zone and celebrate with care,
Show a zest for the holiday fanfare.

Zapped into the world of Christmas baking,
Tarts and zucchini cakes – things to be making.
Party guests try new foods, at least just a bite,
Hosts feel like zombies after sleepless nights.

Christmas is a time to show love with zest,
But it should not be a competition or contest.
When at a Christmas party, try to unwind,
Zing with a person who shares your Zodiac sign.

Christmas meals with our caring folks,
Filled with funny zingers and jokes.
Zonked on the couch at the end of the night,
Bye to the guests as they head out of sight.

Time for a zesty hot chocolate - rather milky and nice,
As the hockey Zamboni on the TV cleans up the ice.
Thinking about other things you can do,
As the season of festivities awaits you.

Alberta's Calgary Zoo hosts Zoolights each year,
Spreading much Christmas magic and holiday cheer.
1.5 million beautiful lights fill the Zoo,
Skate the ice rink with music or make an igloo.

Before your next poem, before the next page in the book,
Can you spot the words with "Z"? – Will you take a good look?
There are *zoom*, *zip*, and *zany* to name but a few,
Zigzag, *zone*, and *Zamboni* are on that list too.

To Learn More

Letter A
For more information on:
- Alberta - See https://www.travelalberta.com/ca/
- Alberta – See http://www.brewsteradventures.com/
- Anne Murray – See http://www.annemurray.com/
- Argentina – See https://kids.nationalgeographic.com/explore/countries/argentina/
- Australia – See http://www.australia.com/en-us
- Avril Lavigne – See http://www.avrillavigne.com/

Letter B
For more information on:
- BeaverTails – See http://beavertails.com/en/about-us/
- Bracebridge - See http://www.bracebridge.ca/en/index.aspx#
- Brampton - See http://www.brampton.ca/en/pages/welcome.aspx
- Burlington – See https://www.burlington.ca/en/index.asp

Letter C
For more information on:
- Capilano Suspension Bridge Park - See https://www.capbridge.com/explore/canyon-lights/
- Casa Loma – See http://www.casaloma.ca/
- Le Chateau Stores – See https://www.lechateau.com/style/company/links/about.jsp
- The CBC – See http://www.cbc.radio-canada.ca/en/explore/our-history/

Letter D
For more information on:
- Dalhousie – See https://www.dal.ca/
- Dalplex – See https://athletics.dal.ca/
- Distillery District – See http://www.thedistillerydistrict.com/
- Downey's Farm – See http://www.downeysfarm.com/

Letter E
For more information on:
- Eaton Centre – See https://www.cfshops.com/toronto-eaton-centre.html
- Edmonton – See https://www.edmonton.ca/
- Eggnog – See http://www.secondcup.com/menu/beverages/Eggnog-latte
- England – See http://www.bbcamerica.com/anglophenia/2012/12/british-up-your-christmas-holiday/
- Europeans & Epiphany – See http://www.catholic.org/news/hf/faith/story.php?id=66407

Letter F
For more information on:
- Feliz Navidad (Christmas in Spain)– See http://www.spain.info/en_CA/
- Fort McMurray – See http://www.fortmcmurraytourism.com/
- Fredericton - See http://www.tourismfredericton.ca/en
- Fredericton – Stompin Tom – See http://www.stompintom.com/

Letter G
For more information on:
- Germany - See http://www.germany.travel/en/index.html
- Gift giving & Ed Mirvish – See http://www.cbc.ca/news/canada/toronto/honest-eds-turkeys
- Greece – See http://www.visitgreece.gr/

Letter H
For more information on:
- Halifax – See https://www.halifax.ca/
- Hamilton – See http://tourismhamilton.com/
- Harrods Department Store - See https://www.harrods.com/en-gb
- The Heft – See https://www.theheft.com/
- Hockey Night in Canada – See http://www.cbc.ca/sports/hockey/nhl
- Hudson's Bay – See https://www.thebay.com/

Letter I
For more information on:
- Inuit – See http://www.thecanadianencyclopedia.ca/en/article/inuit/
- Ireland – See http://www.ireland.com/en-ca/
- Italy – See http://www.italia.it/en/home.html

Letter J
For more information on:
- The Fairmont Jasper Park Lodge Hotel – See http://www.fairmont.com/jasper/
- Jacques Cartier – See https://www.quebecregion.com/en/quebec-city-and-area/jacques-cartier/
- Jasper – See https://www.jasper-alberta.com/

Letter K
For more information on:
- Kingston – See https://www.cityofkingston.ca/
- Kitchener – See http://www.explorewaterlooregion.com/region-of-waterloo/city-of-kitchener/

Letter L
For more information on:
- Lake Louise – See https://www.banfflakelouise.com/lake-louise
- Louisbourg– See http://louisbourg.ca/

Letter M
For more information on:
- Mew Lake Campground - See https://www.ontarioparks.com/park/algonquin/mewlake
- Midnight Meal/Noche Buena – See https://kidworldcitizen.org/christmas-in-the-philippines/
- Mount St. Louis Moonstone - See https://mountstlouis.com/
- Muskoka – See http://www.discovermuskoka.ca/things-to-do/

Letter N
For more information on:
- Newfoundland - See http://www.thecanadianencyclopedia.ca/en/article/christmas-in-canada/
- Newfoundland's Bay Roberts – See http://www.bayroberts.com/?page_id=272
- Niagara Falls – See https://www.niagarafallstourism.com/
- Nova Scotia – See http://www.novascotia.com/

Letter O
For more information on:
- Ontario – See https://www.ontariotravel.net/en/home
- Orangeville – See http://orangevilletourism.ca/
- Ottawa, General Tourism – See https://www.ottawatourism.ca/,
  Ottawa's Fairmont Chateau Laurier Hotel – See http://www.fairmont.com/laurier-ottawa/
  Ottawa's Rideau Canal Skateway – See https://rcs.ncc-ccn.ca/

Letter P
For more information on:
- Parade in Toronto – See http://thesantaclausparade.com/
- Polar Bears & Tundra Buggy– See https://www.canadapolarbears.com/subject/polar-bear-tours
- Pyramid Lake & Fat Bikes – See https://mpljasper.com/hotels/pyramid-lake-resort/amenities/

Letter Q
For more information on:
- Quality Street Chocolate – See http://www.qualitystreetchocolates.com/
- Quebec, General Tourism – See https://www.ville.quebec.qc.ca/en/
  Quebec's Cirque Du Soleil – See https://www.cirquedusoleil.com/about/history
  Quebec's Hotel De Glace – See http://www.hoteldeglace-canada.com/
  Quebec's Joseph Bombardier – See https://www.theglobeandmail.com/news/national/canada- 150/great-\canadian-innovations-how-the-snowmobile-opened-much-of canadasnorth/article34590806/
  Quebec's Notre Dame Cathedral – See https://www.quebecregion.com/en/businesses/attractions/religious-sites/notre-dame-de-quebec-basilica-cathedral/
- Queen's Speech – See http://www.bbcamerica.com/anglophenia/2012/12/british-up-your-christmas-holiday

Letter R
For more information on:
- Rockies/Castle in The Rockies – See http://www.fairmont.com/banff-springs/
- Rudolph, The Red Nose Reindeer - See https://www.thestar.com/entertainment/2014/12/09/rudolph_the_rednosed_reindeers_toronto_connection.html

Letter S
For more information on:
- Saskatoon, Saskatchewan – See http://www.tourismsaskatchewan.com/
- Saskatoon, Saskatchewan Statistics - See https://globalnews.ca/news/3425371/census-2016-saskatoon-children-outnumber-seniors-bucking-national-trend/
- Second Cup – See http://www.secondcup.com/
- Shoppers Drug Mart – See https://www1.shoppersdrugmart.ca/en/home
- Simcoe's Panorama River, Ontario – See http://www.simcoepanorama.ca/
- Swiss Chalet – See https://www.swisschalet.com/about-us

Letter T
For more information on:
- Toronto – See http://www.toronto.com/
- Trivial Pursuit – See http://www.nytimes.com/2010/06/03/business/03haney.html

Letter U
For more information on:
- Ukraine – See http://www.traveltoukraine.org/
- U.S.A's Hawaii - See https://www.gohawaii.com/
- U.S.A's Louisiana – See http://www.louisianatravel.com/U.S.A's New England
- U.S.A's New England – See http://www.discovernewengland.org/
- U.S.A's New York City – See https://www.nycgo.com/

Letter V
For more information on:
- Vancouver – See https://www.tourismvancouver.com/
- Via Rail – See http://www.viarail.ca/en
- Village Vacances Valcartier, Québec – See http://www.valcartier.com/en/indoor-waterpark/
- Vocalist – Michael Buble – See http://www.michaelbuble.com/

Letter W
For more information on:
- Waterloo – See http://www.explorewaterlooregion.com/region-of-waterloo/city-of-kitchener/
- West Edmonton Mall – See http://www.wem.ca/
- Whistler – See https://www.whistler.com/
- Winnipeg – See https://www.tourismwinnipeg.com/
- Winter Exhibits – Quebec - See https://carnaval.qc.ca/carnaval/who-is-bonhomme-carnaval
- Winter Exhibits – Yorkville – See http://bloor-yorkville.com/

Letter X
- Exploring Christmas shops – The Spirit Of Christmas Store – See https://www.spiritofchristmas.ca/
- Exploring year-round shops – Just Christmas Store – See http://www.justchristmas.ca/

Letter Y
For more information on:
- Yukon Territories – See https://www.travelyukon.com/
- Yule lads, Iceland – See https://www.inspiredbyiceland.com/
- Yurts in Algonquin Provincial Park – See http://www.algonquinpark.on.ca/visit/camping/mew-lake-campground.php

Letter Z
For more information on:
- Zoolights at The Calgary Zoo – See https://www.calgaryzoo.com/zoolightsyyc

Fun Educational Follow-ups:

Discussion Questions:
1) Did you learn anything new about Christmas? If so, what did you learn?
2) What are some symbols of Christmas that have been discussed?
3) What did you find most interesting?
4) Which country do you and your family come from? Is it featured in this book? If not, what would you say about your culture and your Christmas traditions? How do you celebrate Christmas? What are some symbols of your traditions? What rituals do you participate in at Christmas?
5) Did you have a favourite letter in *The ABCs of Christmas* book? If so, what is it and why?

Activities:
1) **Art:** Do you see primary and secondary colours on the page(s)? Primary colours are red, yellow and blue. Secondary colours are colours you get when you combine two primary colours. Mixing red and blue creates purple. Mixing blue and yellow creates green. Mixing red and yellow creates orange.
2) **Art:** Create a collage for your home or classroom of Christmas symbols from the book (i.e. Use a letter from the book and create a Christmas collage using the symbols mentioned).
3) **Language Arts:** Using the *spot the words* cue after each letter, identify which words are directly related to Christmas. Are these words symbols, traditions, people, places or something else? Explain.
4) **Language Arts:** Find at least three nouns on each page. A noun is a person, place or thing. Write one sentence describing each noun.
5) **Language Arts:** Find at least three adjectives on each page. An adjective is a word that describes a noun. Use the adjectives you have noticed to create an alternate winter or Christmas scene.
6) **Language Arts:** Find at least two verbs on each page. A verb is an action word such as running.
7) **Language Arts:** Create a paragraph to summarize what you have learned from a letter in *The ABCs of Christmas*.
8) **Math:** How many words start with the letter that appears at the top of the page (i.e. How many words start with the letter "A" on the "Letter A" page?).
9) **Math:** How many images or pictures do you see on each page?
10) **Math:** How many interesting country facts are on each page?
11) **Math:** How often do you see the colours red and green throughout the book?
12) **Math:** Is there any symmetry in the book or evidence of patterns? Symmetry is having things balanced with equal weight from the center. A pattern can be a repeated image or design.
13) **Music:** Create a poem, prayer or song with music that is inspired from *The ABCs of Christmas*.
14) **Science:** Describe a place in *The ABCs of Christmas* that has freezing temperatures. How does the Christmas weather in this place compare to the Christmas weather from where you are from?
15) **Science:** Evergreen trees are associated with Christmas. What type of trees do you have in your nieghbourhood and for what are they known?
16) **Technology:** Using a snow-based product innovation or invention mentioned in *The ABCs of Christmas* (i.e. Snowmobile or The Heft), conduct an internet research project using the links provided in the "Learn More" section of the book. Who created this product and how has this product improved the way people live?

Printed in the United States
By Bookmasters